BATH BOMBS,
BATH MELTS,
SCRUBS AND SALTS

TABLE OF CONTENTS

INTRODUCTION

This book contains everything you need to know about bath bombs, melts, scrubs, and salts.

A long, relaxing bath can make you feel pampered. Leave your skin feeling soft and silky, looking younger and well-nourished. The scents also make baths even more luxurious.

The colors, the fizzes and foams also make baths more fun, especially for children.

However, these can be very pricey, luckily you can make your own for much less.

This book will guide you through every step in making these wonderful bath add-ons. You will also learn and understand about each ingredient that goes into your recipes. You will also learn the important safety guidelines for a better bath experience without nasty side effects.

Thanks for purchasing this book, I hope you enjoy it!

CHAPTER 1:

INTRODUCTION TO BATH BOMBS, BATH MELTS, AND BATH SCRUBS

Your bath can be made more luxurious like an expensive spa or health and wellness resort experience. You just need a few simple ingredients to make your own bath bombs, bath melts, bath salts, and bath scrubs.

Bath bombs are hard spheres that fizz, bubble or foam when dropped into a tub of water. These give the bath water scents, bubbles or colors, depending on the ingredients. Most often, these do not leave an oily layer to the bath water. One issue, though, is color. Sometimes, the colors added to the bath bombs can stick to the tub and can be difficult to get rid of.

Bath melts are made with oils, butters and/or waxes. These are melted in a tub of hot water. Soaking in these will leave the skin moisturized, from all the butters/oils/waxes floating in the water. One big issue in using bath melts is the oily layer. This can make the tub slippery.

Bath salts are mixtures added to bath water. These add scent and act as aromatherapy agents for a soothing, relaxing, rejuvenating, skin-friendly bath. The nutrients in the ingredients are released into the bath water when the bath salts are melted. During the bath, these nutrients are absorbed into the skin.

Bath scrubs are applied to wet skin, then rubbed gently. They are used to exfoliate and remove dead skin cells to promote new, softer, and healthier skin cells. These are also used to apply nutrients to the skin. The rubbing motion helps these nutrients to be absorbed into the skin.

The effect of the bath bombs, melts, scrubs, and salts depend on the ingredients. Essential oils, especially, provide the desired scent and effect. For example, lavender promotes a luxurious relaxing effect when used as an ingredient. You may only be adding a few drops, but with good quality essential oil, it will be enough for a nice relaxing bath.

Safety precautions

Safe use makes for great experience with these recipes. Here are some you need to know:

1. Use one bomb per tub.

   Using too much in a bath creates a concentrated mixture of ingredients in the bath water. This can lead to irritation. More in this case is not always good for the body.

   Be careful in getting in and out of the tub.

   The added oils in these products can make the bath tub more slippery. Always be careful.

   Clean the tub before and after use.

   Dirt, as well as soap and oil residue can be great breeding places for molds and mildew. These can get mixed into the water, and create a nasty concoction for your body.

   Cleaning after is also a good way to remove any oils that may have stuck to the tub when the water has drained.

This will reduce breeding grounds for microorganisms, as well as reduce stains from ruining your tub.

2. In using bath teas, steep the tea bags in the tub water as you would with a cup of tea.

Some people also place the tea bag under the tap as it fills the tub with hot water. Keep the tea bags in the tub as you soak in order to get all the beautiful nutrients and scents from the mix.

To make cleaning a lot easier afterwards, keep the tea mixture within its bag when using. This way, you only get to lift the bag out of the tub instead of rinsing away all the herbs all over the tub.

3. Be careful when using with babies and children.

Some ingredients, especially the essential oils, can be highly irritating for some babies and children. Use only oils that are listed as safe for kids.

CHAPTER 2:

EQUIPMENT AND FREQUENTLY USED INGREDIENTS

Making bath bombs, melts, sugars, salts, and scrubs are easy. It does not need any special equipment. However, it is best to use tools and equipment dedicated to these. If this is not economical for you, clean the tools and equipment very well before and after use. This way, you won't be contaminating food when using.

For example, a mold should be dedicated to bath bombs and melts. This is a must if you are using non-food grade ingredients such as soap colorants. Other tools, such as spatulas, and mortar-and-pestle can be used as long as you clean it well before and after use.

However, cleaning may be a bit more tricky when you add the fragrant oils. The fragrances can linger and might get transferred to food. For example, crushing lavender buds in a food processor can leave a strong lavender scent that can get infused into food when you use the food processor the next time.

Common tools and equipment

Here is a list of the tools and equipment that you need to have on hand to make any of these recipes:

- Molds

  Silicon molds are great because it is easier to take the bath bombs/melt out once dried or solidified. For bath bombs, there are plastic or metal sphere molds available online or in craft stores to get the iconic bath bomb look.

- Scoops, measuring cups, measuring spoons

  Of course, you need these to get the right amount from containers. Some prefer to use plastic scoops, as some metals may react with the ingredients and cause some unpredictable effects.

- Scales

  These come in handy when you work with butters, waxes, and coconut oil. These ingredients are difficult to pack into measuring cups and spoons and take them out. Weighing these out are much more convenient.

- Gloves

  These help prevent getting your hands colored when mixing liquid and/or powder coloring into your mixtures. You can also use gloves to prevent any irritation when handling ingredients like citric acid and baking soda, especially if you have sensitive skin or cracked hands.

- Mask

  This is a great thing to wear when you handle SLSA. This ingredient is a very fine powder. It is safe but it can disperse in air easily. It can make you cough and sneeze when you inhale it.

Ingredients

This is a short list of the key ingredients in bath bombs. You will also understand exactly what the ingredients do for the recipe and for your skin.

Caution: These ingredients are generally safe for use on the skin. However, some people may have sensitivities to some of these ingredients. In case skin irritation, burning sensation, redness or itchiness are experienced, get out of the bath and rinse the entire body well with clean water. Avoid using these products and seek consultation with a skin expert to assess if further treatment is necessary.

Baking soda

This works hand-in-hand with citric acid. The reaction of these two to water creates the wonderful fizzing effect when the bomb is dropped into the water.

This ingredient can help in managing pH levels in the bath and in the skin. It is a weak alkaline that can help neutralize acidity in the skin. It also has anti-inflammatory and antiseptic benefits that can help with conditions such as mild rashes and minor skin irritations.

Caution: Some people may have a negative reaction to baking soda. It can cause burning sensation, as well as rashes and redness. Use organic baking soda. Also, use baking soda used for cooking, not the commercial-grade one as the commercial-grade can have added ingredients that can cause the irritation.

Citric acid

As mentioned above, citric acid forms a chemical reaction with baking soda and water for the fizzing effect.

It also promotes the removal of dead skin cells. This promotes faster skin cell turnover for healthier, new skin cells. This can help improve minor wrinkles, as well as even out skin tone and texture.

Caution: Too much citric acid can be irritating to the skin. It can cause burning and stinging sensation, as well as skin irritation. Some people may also have higher sensitivity to citric acid.

Cornstarch

Some recipes call for addition of cornstarch. The effect is slowing down the fizzing or bubbling when the bath bomb combines with water.

This is an amazing natural ingredient that can help with many skin issues. It can help soothe skin irritations such as skin allergies and sunburns. It also leaves a silky feel to the skin after a nice bath soak.

Castor or Vegetable Oil

These act as binders for bath bombs. In melts, sugar scrubs and salts, these can be used to add more benefits to the bath. These are also used as carrier oils for essential oils added into the recipe.

As carrier oils, they serve to dilute the essential oils to reduce the possibility of skin irritation.

Essential oils

These add scent and benefits to the bath. Use high grade essential oils. Check the source and the labels to make sure that the essential oil is pure and does not contain any harmful additives.

Caution: These will come in contact with the skin and some sensitive parts such as the mucus membranes of the genital area and the anus, as well as the nose and sensitive skin in the face and even in the eyes. Some people may be sensitive to the oils. High concentration of essential oils can also be irritating. Dilute with carrier oils and use only in indicated amounts.

Colorants

Always use food grade colorants in the bath bomb, melt, salt and scrub. The color will dissolve in water and will get in contact with the skin. Most non-food grade colorings have not been tested for safety for use on skin. This can be a likely source of irritation.

Some recipes call for liquid colorants, while others call for powders. It depends on your preference. However, it is important to note the effect on the ratio of wet to dry ingredients. You may need to adjust the moisture you add to the recipe if you wish to use liquid colorant over the powder called for. On the other hand, you may need to add a bit more moisture, such as a small spray of water or witch hazel if you substitute powder colorant to the liquid called for in the recipe.

Glitters and mica powder

These ingredients give the bath bomb, melt, salt, scrub and the water a nice color. Choose cosmetic grade glitters and mica powder for reduced chances of skin irritation. Do not use glitters used in art crafts as these may be too large or too rough for the skin.

Fragrances

Some recipes require the addition of fragrances. Make sure that the fragrance oil you use is non toxic. Some fragrances may contain harmful ingredients such as benzene derivatives and phthalates. Check the label. Best to choose organic fragrance blends.

Notes on using salts

Many of the recipes here call for salts, not just in bath salts but in some bath scrubs and bombs as well. Here's a short guide to help you understand salts better.

Epsom salts

This is not salt in the way most of us consider salt. Epsom salt is actually magnesium sulfate. It is a chemical compound consisting of magnesium, oxygen and sulfur molecules.

This has many health benefits, including detoxification and it is a rich source of skin-friendly nutrients.

Himalayan Pink salt

This is another nutrient-rich ingredient that can help nourish the skin. The trace minerals and elements in this salt can have a nice anti-inflammatory effect for relief of skin irritation.

Dead Sea salt

Using this can give the bath more nutrients. This can help in replenishing the skin with important minerals for relaxing and softening the skin. It also contains sulfur that can help treat certain skin conditions such as eczema and acne.

Notes on herbs and essential oils

Use this list as a guide on the effects of herbs and essential oils that you may want to add into your recipes:

Chamomile

- Calming
- Relaxing
- Promotes sleep
- Relieves stress

Lavender

- Calming
- Relaxing
- Soothing on irritated skin
- Antimicrobial effect
- Uplifts mood for aromatherapy

Rose

- Soothing on irritated skin
- Cooling
- Astringent properties
- Uplifting scent

Rose petals

- Soften the skin
- Refreshes
- Relaxes

Comfrey

- Soothes skin inflammation
- Promotes wound healing
- Soothes rashes

Oats

- Calms skin redness
- Soothes irritations and itchiness
- Leaves skin feeling silky and soft

Cacao/cocoa butter

- Serves as emollient
- Rich in vitamin E
- Hydrates the skin

Green tea, coffee

- Detox
- Relaxation
- Antioxidant

Jasmine

- Refreshes skin
- Enhances mood

Grated ginger

- Improve blood circulation to the skin

Calendula

- Soothes
- Relaxes
- Softens the skin

Thyme, rosemary

- Relaxes

Mint, lemongrass, basil

- Supports skin healing

Eucalyptus

- Relaxes

Hibiscus

- Anti-inflammatory

CHAPTER 3:

BATH BOMB RECIPES

WHITE MILK BATH BOMB

INGREDIENTS:

- 1/2 cup cornstarch
- 1/3 cup powdered milk
- 1/4 cup sea salt
- 1 cup baking soda
- 3/4 citric acid
- 1 tbsp almond oil
- 1 tbsp grape seed oil
- 1 tbsp cocoa butter
- 1 tbsp shea butter
- Witch hazel in a spray bottle

DIRECTIONS:

1. Mix all the dry ingredients thoroughly.
2. Melt the butters.
3. Stir in the oils into the melted butters.
4. Pour butter-oil mixture into the dry mixture. Combine thoroughly.
5. Check the consistency.
6. Add one spray witch hazel and mix thoroughly. Gradually add one spray at a time to get the right consistency.
7. Pack the mixture into the mold tightly. Allow to dry for 24 hours before removing.
8. Place bombs in a sealed container and allow to dry fully.

CHAMPAGNE SALT BATH BOMB

INGREDIENTS:

- 1 cup baking soda
- 1/2 cup cornstarch
- 1/2 cup dead sea salt
- 1/2 cup citric acid
- 2 1/2 tbsp light vegetable oil
- 2 tsp grapefruit essential oil
- 1 drop pink food coloring

DIRECTIONS:

1. Blend all the dry ingredients well in a mixing bowl, removing any clumps.
2. Mix all the liquids in a separate bowl.
3. Slowly pour the liquid mixture into the dry mixture, stirring frequently to combine well.
4. Pack the mixture into the molds. Set aside to dry for 24-48 hours.
5. Remove from mold and store in a sealed container to continue drying fully.

BUTTERY YLANG-YLANG BATH BOMB

INGREDIENTS:

- 1 cup baking soda
- 1/2 cup citric acid
- 1/2 cup grated cocoa butter
- Musk fragrance oil
- Ylang ylang essential oil
- Witch hazel in a spray bottle

DIRECTIONS:

1. Combine baking soda and citric acid in a bowl into an even, clump-free mixture.
2. Mix fragrance oil and essential oil then pour into the dry mixture slowly.
3. Mix well to distribute the oils.
4. Spray the mixture once with witch hazel. Mix well and check consistency.
5. Add one spray gradually and mix well before checking consistency. Once right consistency is achieved, pack the mixture into the molds.
6. Set aside to dry for 24 hours before unmolding.

MILKY CALENDULA BATH BOMB

INGREDIENTS:

- 1/3 cup Epsom salts
- 1/4 cup powdered milk
- 1 tsp essential oil
- 2 tsp melted cocoa butter
- 2 tbsp olive oil
- Calendula petals
- Witch hazel in a spray bottle

DIRECTIONS:

1. Combine all the dry ingredients well.
2. Mix all the liquid ingredients together in a separate bowl.
3. Pour the liquid mixture gradually into the dry mixture, mixing continuously to keep the mixture from fizzing.
4. Mix well until the mixture is uniformly combined. Break down any lumps.
5. Spray the mixture once with witch hazel and mix thoroughly.
6. Check the consistency.
7. Spray a little gradually as need to get the right consistency.
8. Pack tightly into the molds and set aside to dry for 24 hours to harden.
9. Unmold and store in a sealed container to fully dry.

OAT-AND-SALT BATH BOMB

INGREDIENTS:

- 1 cup baking soda
- 1/2 cup ground oatmeal
- 1/2 cup citric acid
- 1/2 cup Epsom salt
- Witch hazel in a spray bottle
- 4 tbsp coconut oil
- 1 tsp essential oil of your choice

DIRECTIONS:

1. Combine all the dry ingredients in a mixing bowl. Make sure to break down all the clumps.
2. Mix oils in a separate bowl.
3. Slowly pour the oil mixture into the dry mixture and mix thoroughly.
4. Spray the mixture with witch hazel once and mix well.
5. Check the consistency. Spray bit by bit, mixing well before spraying to get the right consistency.
6. Pack tightly into molds and set aside to dry for 1-2 days.

APRICOT AND OATMEAL BATH BOMB

INGREDIENTS:

- 2 tbsp cornstarch
- 2 tbsp citric acid
- 1/4 cup oatmeal
- 1/4 cup baking soda
- 5 drops orange food coloring
- 10 drops of tea tree essential oil
- 1 1/2 tbsp apricot oil
- Witch hazel in a spray bottle

DIRECTIONS:

1. Mix all dry ingredients well.
2. Slowly stir in apricot oil and essential oil into the mixture. Mix well.
3. Spray once with witch hazel. Mix thoroughly then check consistency.
4. Add a little bit more water to get the right consistency.
5. Pack tightly into molds.
6. Set aside to dry for 1-2 days.

FRENCH MACARON BATH BOMBS

INGREDIENTS:

- 1/2 cup Epsom salts
- 1 cup baking soda
- 1/2 cup citric acid
- 1/2 cup cornstarch
- 3 tbsp baby oil

For the filling:

- 1 cup baking soda

- A few drops of different gel food coloring
- Witch hazel in a spray bottle

- 1/4 cup cocamidopropyl betaine

DIRECTIONS:

1. Mix the first 4 dry ingredients well.
2. Add baby oil and mix.
3. If doing several colors from this single batch, divide the mixture then add a few gel colors to each batch, depending on desired color vibrancy. Mix well after adding the gel.
4. Spray once with witch hazel then mix well. Check the consistency. Spray once more to get the right consistency.
5. Pack the macaron molds tightly with the mixture.
6. Flatten the top and place a cookie sheet over the molds and carefully flip the mold.
7. Tap the mold gently to release the bath bombs.
8. Carefully transfer the bath macarons on wax paper resting on a soft towel to dry for 24 hours.
9. Once dry, mix baking soda and cocamidopropyl betaine for the filling. The mixture is a paste, mashed potato-like consistency. Put in a piping bag and squeeze to fill the

underside of one macaron. Place one unfilled macaron over the filling and gently squeeze to put them together.

10. Dry the assembled macaron fully for a few hours.

CUPCAKE BATH BOMBS

INGREDIENTS:

- 1/4 cup citric acid
- 1 cup Epsom salt
- 2 1/2 cup baking soda
- Pink food coloring
- Witch hazel in a spray bottle
- Meringue frosting

DIRECTIONS:

1. Mix all the dry ingredients well.
2. Stir in the coloring and essential oils. Mix well.
3. Spray once with witch hazel. Mix and check consistency. Add small sprays as needed to get the right consistency.
4. Put liners into the pan. Fill each liner and let it sit overnight to dry.
5. To get the classic cupcake look, make meringue frosting and pipe on top. Set aside to dry.

MERMAID SHELL BATH BOMBS

INGREDIENTS:

- 1 cup baking soda
- 1/2 cup citric acid
- 1/2 tsp olive oil
- 1-3 drops lavender essential oil
- Witch hazel in a spray bottle
- Neon pink food coloring
- Seashell silicone mold
- Pearl candy
- White foam shaving cream

DIRECTIONS:

1. Blend all the dry ingredients well.
2. Blend in the essential oils.
3. Stir in olive oil until evenly combined.
4. Put 3 drops of food coloring and mix well to evenly distribute color. Add more gradually if you want a deeper color.
5. Spray the mixture once with witch hazel. Mix well and check the consistency.
6. Press the mixture firmly into the mold.
7. Set aside to dry overnight.
8. Carefully remove the bath bombs from the mold. Set aside in a sealed container to fully dry.
9. Once fully dry, put some shaving cream on one bath bomb and press another on top to seal. Press a pearl candy in between to look like a pearl poking out of an oyster.

MIDAS TOUCH BATH BOMBS

INGREDIENTS:

- 1 1/2 cups citric acid
- 3 cups baking soda
- 7 ml champagne fragrance oil
- 1.5 oz meadowfoam oil
- 1/2 tbsp orange peel fragrance oil
- 2 tbsp cocoa butter
- Gold mica
- 10-12 drops coral orange food coloring
- 99% isopropyl alcohol in a spray bottle
- Witch hazel in a spray bottle

DIRECTIONS:

1. Combine baking soda and citric acid in a bowl.
2. Put cocoa butter and meadowfoam oil in a small microwaveable bowl. Microwave in short 30-second burst until butter is melted. Cool slightly.
3. Pour the oil-butter mixture into the dry mixture. Stir thoroughly to evenly combine everything.
4. Add the color. Mix to distribute the color evenly.
5. Add the 2 fragrance oils and mix it in thoroughly.
6. Check the consistency. Spray the mixture once with witch hazel and mix well.
7. Adjust the moisture one spray at a time to get the right consistency.
8. Fill the molds then press them together tightly.
9. Allow to dry for 24 hours.
10. Unmold.
11. Spray the entire surface lightly with isopropyl alcohol.

12. Dip the bombs immediately on the gold mica to coat. Work fast as the alcohol evaporates quickly, making it hard for mica to stick to the bombs.
13. Dry the bombs.
14. Put bombs back into the mold.
15. Remove only when ready to use.

SPACE BATH BOMBS

INGREDIENTS:

- 1 cup baking soda
- 1/2 cup corn starch
- 1/2 cup citric acid
- 3 tbsp Epsom salt
- 2 tsp sweet almond oil
- 3 drops red mandarin essential oil
- 4 drops lavender essential oil
- 2 drop chamomile essential oil
- 2 drop sandalwood essential
- 2 drop marjoram essential oil
- Water in a spray bottle
- Silver pearl dust

DIRECTIONS:

1. Brush the mold with a layer of silver pearl dust.
2. Mix salt, cornstarch, citric acid, and baking soda. A small amount of silver pearl dust can give the mixture a light grey color, if preferred.
3. Mix until there are no more lumps.
4. Mix essential oils, water, and almond oil in a separate bowl.
5. Slowly pour the oil mixture into the dry mixture, stirring continuously.
6. Mix until evenly combined.
7. Check consistency.
8. Lightly spray with water if the mixture doesn't hold its shape.
9. Press the mixture into the prepared star molds.
10. Dry the bombs overnight.
11. Unmold.

SINUS AND COLDS RELIEF BATH BOMBS

INGREDIENTS:

- 1/2 cup citric acid
- 1 cup baking soda
- 3 tbsp Epsom salt
- 1/2 cup corn starch
- 1 tbsp coconut oil
- 10 drops eucalyptus essential oil
- 10 drops peppermint essential oil
- Witch hazel in a spray bottle
- Green food coloring

DIRECTIONS:

1. Mix all the dry ingredients in a bowl.
2. Mix in coconut oil. Break down any lumps.
3. Divide the mixture between 2 bowls. Add eucalyptus oil to one bowl. Add peppermint oil to the other bowl. Mix well.
4. Stir in green coloring to the peppermint mixture. Mix to evenly distribute the color.
5. Spray the mixture with witch hazel. Mix well after each spray.
6. Check the consistency. Adjust to get the right wet sand form.
7. Pack the mixtures in alternate layers in the mold.
8. Allow to dry overnight.
9. Unmold.
10. Store in a sealed container.

COCONUT PEPPERMINT BATH BOMB SNOWBALLS

INGREDIENTS:

- 1/2 cup citric acid
- 1 cup baking soda
- 3 tbsp Epsom salt
- 1/2 cup corn starch
- 1 tbsp coconut oil
- 1 1/2 tsp coconut extract
- 10 drops peppermint essential oil
- Witch hazel in a spray bottle
- Snowflake sugar decorations

DIRECTIONS:

1. Mix all the dry ingredients well.
2. Stir in coconut oil.
3. Mix well to evenly distribute the oil throughout the mixture.
4. Stir in the extract and essential oil. Mix well.
5. Spray 5 times with witch hazel. Mix well and check consistency. Add small sprays as needed to get the right consistency.
6. Put one snowflake into the mold then pack it tightly with the bath bomb mixture.
7. Press the two halves of the mold tightly together. Set aside to dry.
8. Unmold.

CARAMEL APPLE BATH BOMB

INGREDIENTS:

- 1/2 cup citric acid
- 1 cup baking soda
- 3 tbsp Epsom salt
- 1/2 cup corn starch
- 1 tbsp coconut oil
- 5 drops vanilla oil
- 5 drops apple oil
- Witch hazel in a spray bottle
- Apple icing decorations
- Green food coloring
- Royal icing

DIRECTIONS:

1. Mix all the dry ingredients well.
2. Stir in the coconut oil.
3. Mix well to evenly distribute the oil throughout the mixture.
4. Stir in food coloring.
5. Mix well.
6. Add the scents.
7. Mix well.
8. Spray once with witch hazel.
9. Mix well.
10. Check consistency. Add small sprays as needed to get the right consistency.
11. Fill the molds.
12. Press the two halves of the mold tightly together. Set aside to dry for 1-2 hours in the freezer or room temperature overnight.
13. Unmold.
14. Squeeze a small amount of icing at the back of the apple decorations then stick onto the bath bombs.

COCONUT OIL BATH BOMBS

INGREDIENTS:

- 1 cup baking soda
- 1/2 cup cornstarch
- 1/2 cup citric acid
- 1/2 cup Epsom salt
- 1 tsp almond oil
- 3 tbsp melted coconut oil, divided
- 2-3 drops green food coloring
- 2-3 drops pink food coloring
- 2-3 drops yellow food coloring

DIRECTIONS:

1. Mix all the dry ingredients well. Divide between 3 bowls.
2. Mix 1 tbsp melted coconut oil and 2-3 drops of green coloring.
3. Add 1/3 tsp of almond oil.
4. Stir this oil mixture into one of the bowls of dry mixture.
5. Mix well to evenly distribute the oil throughout the mixture.
6. Repeat with the other 2 colors and bowls.
7. Pack the molds tightly with the mixture, alternating layers of colors.
8. Press the two halves of the mold tightly together. Put in the freezer to set for 20 minutes.
9. Unmold.

ALLERGY RELIEF BATH BOMBS

INGREDIENTS:

- 1 cup baking soda
- 1/2 cup corn starch
- 1/2 cup citric acid
- 3 tbsp Epsom salt
- 8-10 drops lemon oil
- 8-10 drops lavender oil
- 1 tbsp coconut oil
- Yellow food coloring
- Purple food coloring
- Witch hazel in a spray bottle

DIRECTIONS:

1. Mix all the dry ingredients well.
2. Stir in the coconut oil.
3. Mix well to evenly distribute the oil throughout the mixture.
4. Divide the mixture between two bowls.
5. Add lavender oil in one bowl. Mix well.
6. Add lemon oil in the other bowl. Mix well.
7. Check the consistency.
8. Spray once with witch hazel as needed to get the right consistency.
9. Pack half of the mold tightly with the lemon mixture.
10. Pack the other with the lavender mixture.
11. Press the two halves of the mold tightly together. Set aside to dry.
12. Unmold.

PUMPKIN SPICE BATH BOMB

INGREDIENTS:

- 1/2 cup corn starch
- 1 cup baking soda
- 3 tbsp Epsom salt
- 1/2 cup citric acid
- 1 tbsp coconut oil
- 1 tbsp pumpkin pie spice
- 10 drops vanilla essential oil
- Red food coloring
- Yellow food coloring
- Witch hazel in a spray bottle

DIRECTIONS:

1. Mix all the dry ingredients.
2. Stir in the coconut oil. Distribute it evenly through the mixture.
3. Divide the mixture between 2 bowls.
4. Stir in the pumpkin pie spice to one bowl thoroughly.
5. Add the orange coloring. Mix evenly.
6. Add the vanilla scent to the other bowl.
7. Mix well to evenly distribute the oil throughout the mixture.
8. Spray 5 times with witch hazel. Mix well.
9. Check consistency. Add small sprays as needed to get the right consistency.
10. Do the same with the other bowl.
11. Pack the molds tightly, layering alternately with the 2 mixtures.
12. Press the two halves of the mold tightly together.
13. Set aside to dry 1 hour in freezer or room temperature overnight.
14. Unmold.

PUMPKIN SPICE MACARON BATH BOMBS

INGREDIENTS:

- 3/4 cup baking soda
- 1/2 cup citric acid
- 1 cup cornstarch
- 5 drops body-safe pumpkin spice oil mixed with a little melted coconut oil or pinch of pumpkin pie spice
- Orange food coloring
- Water in a spray bottle

DIRECTIONS:

1. Combine all the dry ingredients, including the color and pumpkin spice oil-coconut oil mixture thoroughly.
2. Spray with water once, mix well and check consistency. Spray once again, to adjust if necessary.
3. Pack the mixture tightly into the mold. Keep extra mixture in a sealed container.
4. Let it dry for 30-60 minutes.
5. Remove the bath bombs from the mold.
6. Put a small amount of unused mixture on top of one bomb and press another bomb on top of it to form the macaron look. Dry for a few more minutes.

SEAWEED BATH BOMBS

INGREDIENTS:

- 1/2 cup citric acid
- 1 cup baking soda
- 1/2 cup detox bath salt
- 1 tbsp extra-virgin olive oil
- 2 drops yellow food coloring
- 5 drops eucalyptus essential oil
- 5 drops peppermint essential oil
- 1 1/2 tsp water

DIRECTIONS:

1. Combine detox bath salt, citric acid, and baking soda in a bowl.
2. In a separate bowl, mix essential oils, water, and olive oil.
3. Slowly pour the liquid mixture into the dry mixture while mixing constantly.
4. Mix well.
5. Pack the molds tightly with the mixture.
6. Press the two halves of the mold tightly together. Set aside to dry.
7. Unmold.

ORANGESICLE BATH BOMBS

INGREDIENTS:

- 2 tbsp melted shea butter
- 1/4 cup cornstarch
- 1/4 cup citric acid
- 1/2 cup baking soda
- 15 drops sweet orange essential oil
- Few drops orange food coloring
- Witch hazel in a spray bottle

DIRECTIONS:

1. Mix all the dry ingredients, except coloring, together.
2. Stir melted shea butter and essential oil together.
3. Slowly pour the liquid mixture into the dry mixture while mixing constantly.
4. Mix well.
5. Add the coloring. Mix well.
6. Spray once with witch hazel. Mix well.
7. Check consistency. Add small sprays as needed to get the right consistency.
8. Pack popsicle molds tightly with the mixture.
9. Insert a popsicle stick in the middle.
10. Set aside to dry overnight.
11. Unmold.

CITRIC ACID-FREE BATH BOMBS

INGREDIENTS:

- 1 cup baking soda
- 1/2 cup cornstarch
- 1/4 cup cream of tartar
- 1/2 cup Epsom salt
- 2 1/2 tbsp coconut oil
- 2 tsp essential oil
- 1 tbsp water

DIRECTIONS:

1. Mix all the dry ingredients well.
2. In a separate bowl, mix all the liquid ingredients.
3. Slowly pour the liquid mixture into the dry mixture while continuously stirring.
4. Mix well and check consistency.
5. Pack the molds tightly with the mixture.
6. Press the two halves of the mold tightly together.
7. Unmold.
8. Set aside to dry overnight.

LEMON BATH BOMBS

INGREDIENTS:

- 1 cup baking soda
- 1/2 cup citric acid
- Zest from 1 lemon
- 10 drops lemon essential oil
- Witch hazel in a spray bottle

DIRECTIONS:

1. Mix citric acid and baking soda well into a clump-free, even mixture.
2. Add the zest and lemon essential oil.
3. Mix well while spraying with witch hazel.
4. Check consistency. Add small sprays as needed to get the right consistency.
5. Pack the molds tightly with the mixture.
6. Press the two halves of the mold tightly together. Set aside to dry.
7. Unmold.

TURMERIC LATTE BATH BOMBS

INGREDIENTS:

- 1 cup baking soda
- 1/4 cup cornstarch
- 1 cup citric acid powder
- 1/4 cup coconut milk powder
- 2 tbsp turmeric
- 3 tbsp melted coconut oil or sweet almond oil
- 15 drops jasmine absolute
- 15 drops vanilla essential oil
- 1 tsp iron oxide powder, as colorant
- 1 tbsp water

DIRECTIONS:

1. Mix all the dry ingredients well, including iron oxide powder.
2. In a separate bowl, mix all the liquid ingredients.
3. Slowly pour the liquid mixture into the dry mixture while continuously stirring.
4. Mix well and check consistency.
5. Pack the molds tightly with the mixture.
6. Press the two halves of the mold tightly together.
7. Unmold.
8. Set aside to dry overnight.

DOUGHNUT BATH BOMBS

INGREDIENTS:

- 1/2 cup corn starch
- 1 cup baking soda
- 3 tbsp Epsom salt
- 1/2 cup citric acid
- Light brown food coloring
- Pink food coloring
- 3 tsp melted coconut oil
- 5 drops jelly doughnut fragrance oil
- 15 drops vanilla essential oil
- Witch hazel in a spray bottle
- 2/3 cup Goat's milk soap base
- Sprinkles

DIRECTIONS:

1. Mix all the dry ingredients well.
2. In a separate bowl, mix all the oils.
3. Slowly pour the liquid mixture into the dry mixture while continuously stirring.
4. Mix well to evenly distribute the oil throughout the mixture.
5. Divide the mixture between 2 bowls.
6. Add color to each bowl. Mix well.
7. Spray 2-3 times with witch hazel. Mix well and check consistency. Add small sprays as needed to get the right consistency.
8. Mist the doughnut mold lightly with non-stick spray.
9. Pack half of the mold with pink mixture for the "top" of the doughnut. Fill the rest of the mold with the brown mixture for the body of the doughnut. Scrape off excess.
10. Allow to dry for 8-24 hours.
11. Unmold.

12. Melt the soap base. Cool slightly.
13. Dip the tops of the doughnut bath bombs then put some sprinkles on top.
14. Allow to set at room temperature for 15 minutes.
15. Store in a sealed container.

BUBBLE BAR BATH BOMBS

INGREDIENTS:

- 1/2 cup baking soda
- 1/4 cup corn starch
- 1/4 cup citric acid
- 1-3 tsp bubble bath

DIRECTIONS:

1. Mix all the dry ingredients well.
2. Slowly stir in bubble bath.
3. Mix well to evenly distribute throughout the mixture.
4. Check consistency.
5. Add another teaspoon bubble bath if the mixture doesn't hold its shape.
6. Check consistency.
7. Fill the molds loosely but overfilled with the mixture.
8. Press the two halves of the mold tightly together.
9. Unmold.
10. Set aside to dry for 8-12 hours.

RAINBOW SHERBET SURPRISE BATH FIZZIES

INGREDIENTS:

- 3 cups baking soda
- 1 1/2 cups citric acid
- 1 1/2 cups arrowroot powder
- 4 tbsp melted shea butter
- 3 tbsp energy fragrance oil
- 3 tbsp melted jojoba oil
- 1/3 tsp 99% alcohol
- Water in a spray bottle
- 2-3 tsp green food coloring

DIRECTIONS:

1. Mix all the dry ingredients well.
2. In a separate bowl, mix shea butter and jojoba oil.
3. In another bowl, mix water, fragrance oil, and alcohol.
4. Combine the two liquids. Add the colorant. Mix well.
5. Slowly pour the liquid mixture into the dry mixture while continuously stirring.
6. Mix well.
7. Check consistency. Adjust with a small spray of water if the mixture is too dry to hold its shape.
8. Fill the molds loosely but overfilled with the mixture.
9. Press the two halves of the mold tightly together.
10. Set aside to dry for 24 hours.

OATS AND ROSEMARY BATH BOMBS

INGREDIENTS:

- 1 1/2 cups baking soda
- 1/2 cup arrowroot powder
- 1/2 cup citric acid
- 1/2 cup ground oats
- 10-15 drops rosemary essential oil
- 1/3 cup melted coconut oil

DIRECTIONS:

1. Mix all the dry ingredients in a bowl.
2. Add essential oil to the bowl.
3. Mix well.
4. Mix in coconut oil slowly. Break down any lumps.
5. Fill the molds loosely but overfilled with the mixture.
6. Press the two halves of the mold tightly together. Set aside to dry.
7. Unmold.

ALOE VERA SOOTHING BATH BOMBS

INGREDIENTS:

- 1/2 cup citric acid
- 1 1/2 cups baking soda
- 1/4 cup white kaolin clay
- 10-15 drops lavender essential oil
- 1/4 cup aloe vera gel or liquid

DIRECTIONS:

1. Mix all the dry ingredients well.
2. Stir in the essential oil.
3. Mix well to evenly distribute the oil throughout the mixture.
4. Slowly pour the aloe vera gel, mixing continuously just until the wet sand consistency is achieved.
5. Fill the molds loosely but overfilled with the mixture.
6. Press the two halves of the mold tightly together. Set aside to dry.
7. Unmold.

HERBAL CHAI TEA BATH BOMBS

INGREDIENTS:

- 1/2 cup citric acid
- 1 cup baking soda
- 1/2 cup Epsom salt
- 1/2 cup arrowroot powder
- 1 tbsp sweet almond oil
- 2 tsp or 1 bag chai tea
- 10-15 drops lemongrass essential oil

DIRECTIONS:

1. Mix all the dry ingredients well.
2. Stir in the essential oil.
3. Mix well to evenly distribute the oil throughout the mixture.
4. Slowly pour the sweet almond oil, mixing continuously just until the wet sand consistency is achieved.
5. Fill the molds loosely but overfilled with the mixture.
6. Press the two halves of the mold tightly together. Set aside to dry.
7. Unmold.

CHAPTER 4:

BATH MELT RECIPES

Recipes here are best measured in terms of ounces and grams instead of tablespoons, cups, etc. This helps get a more accurate measurement and right ratio of the butters and oils.

SHEA BUTTER MOISTURIZING BATH MELT

INGREDIENTS:

- 2.5 oz shea butter
- 1.25 oz solid coconut oil
- 10-20 drops lavender essential oil
- Dried calendula flowers

DIRECTIONS:

1. Place shea butter and coconut oil in a heatproof/microwave-proof container. Heat (double boiler or microwave) until butter and oil melts.
2. Cool slightly.
3. Add lavender essential oil.
4. Stir.
5. Put dried calendula flowers inside the molds.
6. Pour the bath melt mixture enough to just cover the dried flowers.
7. Allow to set, about 20 minutes in the freezer.
8. Take the mold out of the freezer and pour bath melt mixture to fill the mold.
9. Allow to harden, in the freezer or at room temperature.

ROSE-LAVENDER LOVE BATH MELTS

INGREDIENTS:

- 2 oz unrefined cocoa butter
- 4 1/2 tsp sweet almond oil
- 5 drops or 1 soft gel capsule (squeeze the oil out to use) vitamin e oil
- 1 tbsp dried lavender buds and rose petals
- 2 tsp lavender essential oil

DIRECTIONS:

1. Place cocoa butter and sweet almond oil in a heatproof/microwave-proof container. Heat (double boiler or microwave) until butter melts.
2. Cool slightly.
3. Add vitamin e oil and lavender essential oil.
4. Stir.
5. Mix the dried rose petals and lavender buds in a bowl. Put inside the molds.
6. Pour the bath melt mixture over the dried petals.
7. Allow to set, about 20 minutes in the freezer.

MOISTURIZING JOJOBA-LAVENDER BATH MELTS

INGREDIENTS:

- 2 oz cocoa butter
- 2 oz shea butter
- 0.2 oz beeswax, grated or pastilles
- 1 tsp jojoba oil
- 1/4 cup dried lavender buds
- 15 -20 drops lavender essential oil

DIRECTIONS:

1. Place cocoa butter, shea butter, and beeswax in a heatproof/microwave-proof container. Heat (double boiler or microwave) until everything melts.
2. Cool slightly.
3. Add jojoba oil and lavender essential oil.
4. Stir.
5. Put lavender buds inside the molds.
6. Pour the bath melt mixture over the buds.
7. Allow to set at room temperature.
8. Unmold.
9. Store in a sealed glass jar.

FIZZING CINNAMON ORANGE BATH MELTS

INGREDIENTS:

- 6 oz cocoa butter
- 1/3 cup sweet almond oil
- 3/4 cup baking soda
- 1/3 cup citric acid
- 10 drop orange essential oil
- 5 drops cinnamon essential oil

DIRECTIONS:

1. Place cocoa butter in a heatproof/microwave-proof container. Heat (double boiler or microwave) until it melts.
2. Cool slightly.
3. Add sweet almond oil.
4. Mix well.
5. Add the essential oils. Stir well.
6. Cool completely but should still be liquid.
7. Whisk together baking soda and citric acid in a separate bowl.
8. Add the dry mixture into the liquid mixture, mixing continuously.
9. Pour into molds.
10. Allow to harden for a few hours.

FIZZING SCENTED BATH MELTS

INGREDIENTS:

- 1.5 oz cocoa butter
- 10 drops lavender essential oil
- 15 drops sweet orange essential oil
- 3 tbsp baking soda
- 2 tsp cornstarch
- 2 tbsp citric acid
- 1/2 tsp ground dried orange blooms
- 1/2 tsp dried lavender buds

DIRECTIONS:

1. Place cocoa butter in a heatproof/microwave-proof container. Heat (double boiler or microwave) until it melts.
2. Cool slightly.
3. Add essential oils.
4. Mix well.
5. Cool completely but should still be liquid.
6. Whisk together cornstarch, baking soda, and citric acid in a separate bowl.
7. Add the dry mixture into the liquid mixture, mixing continuously.
8. Pour into molds.
9. Allow to harden for a few hours.

COCONUT-WHITE CHOCOLATE BATH MELTS

INGREDIENTS:

- 2 oz coconut oil
- 2 oz cacao butter
- 5 drops sweet orange essential oils

DIRECTIONS:

1. Place cocoa butter in a heatproof/microwave-proof container. Heat (double boiler or microwave) until melted.
2. Remove from heat.
3. Stir in coconut oil.
4. Mix until everything is melted and blended well.
5. Cool slightly.
6. Add sweet orange essential oil.
7. Stir thoroughly.
8. Fill the mold with bath melt mixture.
9. Allow to harden, in the freezer or at room temperature.

LAVENDER-CHOCOLATE BATH MELTS

INGREDIENTS:

- 7 oz unrefined cocoa butter
- 4 1/2 cup white granulated sugar
- 8 oz basic white MP soap base
- 8 ml chocolate lavender fragrance oil
- 1 tbsp lavender buds

DIRECTIONS:

1. Place cocoa butter in a heatproof/microwave-proof container. Heat (double boiler or microwave) until melted.
2. Cool slightly.
3. Add fragrance oil.
4. Stir thoroughly.
5. Cool to 120 degrees F.
6. Add sugar.
7. Stir well.
8. Fill the mold with bath melt mixture.
9. Allow to harden, in the freezer or at room temperature.
10. Unmold.
11. Melt the soap base. Cool to 140 degrees F.
12. Dip the bath melts in the melted soap base.
13. Place bath melts on a soft towel.
14. Press lavender buds onto the surface dipped in soap base.
15. Allow to set.

CHOCOLATE-OATMEAL BATH MELTS

INGREDIENTS:

- 4 oz shea butter
- 1 tsp chocolate fragrance oil
- 6 tbsp ground oatmeal
- 4 tbsp citric acid
- 1/2 cup baking soda

DIRECTIONS:

1. Mix the dry ingredients.
2. Place shea butter in a heatproof/microwave-proof container. Heat (double boiler or microwave) until butter and oil melts.
3. Cool slightly.
4. Add chocolate fragrance oil.
5. Stir thoroughly.
6. Carefully put the dry mixture into liquid mixture. Mix while adding.
7. Fill the mold with bath melt mixture.
8. Allow to harden, in the freezer or at room temperature.

DELICIOUS CHERRY-CHOCOLATE BATH MELTS

INGREDIENTS:

- 6.5 oz tucuma butter
- 6.5 oz cocoa butter
- 1 oz ultra-refined beeswax
- 10 ml polysorbate 80
- 3 tsp cocoa powder
- 2 ml black cherry fragrance oil
- 1/2 tsp red mica powder

DIRECTIONS:

1. Place tucuma butter, cocoa butter, and beeswax in a heatproof/microwave-proof container. Heat (double boiler or microwave) until butter and oil melts.
2. Add black cherry fragrance oil and polysorbate 80.
3. Stir thoroughly.
4. Stir in cocoa powder.
5. Mix well.
6. Fill the mold with bath melt mixture.
7. Allow to harden, in the freezer or at room temperature.

PINK CHIFFON BATH MELTS

INGREDIENTS:

- 4 oz tucuma butter
- 4 oz avocado butter blend
- 1/2 cup citric acid powder
- 1 cup baking soda
- 1 tsp white kaolin clay
- 1/8 tsp red food coloring
- 3 ml pink chiffon fragrance oil

DIRECTIONS:

1. Mix citric acid and baking soda.
2. Stir in red color and kaolin clay.
3. Place tucuma butter in a heatproof/microwave-proof container. Heat (double boiler or microwave) until melted.
4. Remove from heat and stir in avocado butter. Stir until everything is melted and well blended.
5. Add fragrance oil.
6. Stir thoroughly.
7. Carefully put the dry mixture into liquid mixture. Mix while adding.
8. Fill the mold with bath melt mixture.
9. Allow to harden in the freezer for 15 minutes.

TROPICAL CITRUS BATH MELTS

INGREDIENTS:

- 9 oz coconut oil
- 10 drops lime essential oil
- 10 drops sweet orange essential oil
- 2 tbsp dried orange peel
- 2 tbsp dried lemon peel

DIRECTIONS:

1. Place coconut oil in a heatproof/microwave-proof container. Heat (double boiler or microwave) until everything melts.
2. Cool slightly.
3. Add the citrus essential oils.
4. Stir.
5. Crush the dried peels into smaller bits.
6. Put dried peels inside the molds.
7. Pour the bath melt mixture over the peel.
8. Allow to set at room temperature.
9. Unmold.
10. Store in a sealed glass jar.

COFFEE BATH MELTS

INGREDIENTS:

- 4 cups baking soda
- 1/3 cup SLSA
- 2 cups citric acid
- 1 tbsp dry coffee grounds
- 2.5 oz cocoa butter wafers
- 0.3 oz vanilla select fragrance oil
- 0.7 oz espresso fragrance oil
- 1 oz coffee seed oil
- 0.5 oz polysorbate 80
- Witch hazel in a spray bottle
- Whole coffee beans

DIRECTIONS:

1. Mix baking soda and citric acid. Break any lumps.
2. Handle the very fine SLSA powder very carefully. Add into the dry mixture and stir slowly to blend well.
3. Place cocoa butter wafers and coffee seed oil in a heatproof/microwave-proof container. Heat (double boiler or microwave) until melted.
4. Remove from heat
5. Stir in polysorbate 80, vanilla select fragrance oil and espresso fragrance oil. Stir until everything is melted and well blended.
6. Stir thoroughly.
7. Carefully pour half of the liquid mixture into the dry mixture. Mix while adding.
8. Continue to slowly pour the rest of the liquid mixture into the bath melt mixture.
9. Mix well.
10. Put a few coffee beans into the mold.
11. Fill the mold with bath melt mixture.
12. Allow to harden in the freezer for 15 minutes.
13. Unmold.

LAVENDER-HONEY RELAXING BATH MELTS

INGREDIENTS:

- 1.8 oz cocoa butter
- 1.8 oz shea butter
- 1/4 tsp honey lavender organic herbal tea
- 30 drops lavender essential oil
- 1 tsp dried lavender flowers

DIRECTIONS:

1. Place cocoa butter and shea butter in a heatproof/microwave-proof container. Heat (double boiler or microwave) until melted.
2. Remove from heat.
3. Open the tea and stir in the contents into the melted butters.
4. Stir in the dried lavender flowers.
5. Put 2 drops of essential oil into the mold.
6. Carefully pour the mixture into the molds.
7. Set aside for the bath melts to fully harden.
8. Unmold.
9. Store in a sealed container, away from heat source.

HONEY-OATMEAL SKIN NOURISHING BATH MELTS

INGREDIENTS:

- 2 oz oat oil
- 4 oz cocoa butter
- 1/3 cup medium sea salt
- 1/2 cup sifted oatmeal, milk, and honey powder base
- 1/4 tsp gold mica powder
- 1/4 tsp roman chamomile essential oil

DIRECTIONS:

1. Place cocoa butter in a heatproof/microwave-proof container. Heat (double boiler or microwave) until melted.
2. Remove from heat.
3. Stir in oat oil.
4. Whisk in powder base.
5. Add essential oil. Mix well.
6. Toss the gold mica powder and the sea salt using a separate bowl.
7. Place the salt-mica mixture inside the molds.
8. Pour the melt mixture into the molds.
9. Set aside for the bath melts to harden fully, in the freezer for 1 hour or a few hours at room temperature.
10. Unmold.
11. Store in a sealed container, away from heat source.

TROPICAL MOJITO BATH MELTS

INGREDIENTS:

- 2 cups coconut oil
- 15 drops peppermint essential oil
- 20 drops lime essential oil
- Zest from 1 lime

DIRECTIONS:

1. Place coconut oil in a heatproof/microwave-proof container. Heat (double boiler or microwave) until melted.
2. Remove from heat.
3. Stir in essential oils. Mix well.
4. Place the zest inside the molds.
5. Pour the melt mixture into the molds.
6. Set aside for the bath melts to harden fully, in the freezer for 1 hour or a few hours at room temperature.
7. Unmold.
8. Store in a sealed container, away from heat source.

DETOXIFYING CEDARWOOD VANILLA BATH MELTS

INGREDIENTS:

- 1 cup coconut oil
- 20 drops cedarwood essential oil
- 10 drops vanilla oil
- 1 tsp black tea

DIRECTIONS:

1. Place coconut oil in a heatproof/microwave-proof container. Heat (double boiler or microwave) until melted.
2. Remove from heat.
3. Stir in essential oils. Mix well.
4. Place bits of the tea inside the molds.
5. Pour the melt mixture into the molds.
6. Set aside for the bath melts to harden fully, in the freezer for 1 hour or a few hours at room temperature.
7. Unmold.
8. Store in a sealed container, away from heat source.

MINTY LEMONGRASS BATH MELTS

INGREDIENTS:

- 1 cup coconut oil
- 8 drops lemongrass essential oi
- 8 drops mint oil
- 1/2 tsp crushed dried lemongrass leaves
- 1/2 tsp crushed dried mint leaves

DIRECTIONS:

1. Place coconut oil in a heatproof/microwave-proof container. Heat (double boiler or microwave) until melted.
2. Remove from heat.
3. Stir in essential oils. Mix well.
4. Mix the dried herbs.
5. Place bits of the herb mixture inside the molds.
6. Pour the melt mixture into the molds.
7. Set aside for the bath melts to harden fully, in the freezer for 1 hour or a few hours at room temperature.
8. Unmold.
9. Store in a sealed container, away from heat source.

SKIN-CLEANSING GRAPEFRUIT BATH MELTS

INGREDIENTS:

- 2 oz organic cocoa butter
- 1/2 oz almond oil
- 2 drops grapefruit essential oil per melt
- 2 drops tangerine essential oil per melt
- Crushed dried grapefruit peel

DIRECTIONS:

1. Place cocoa butter in a heatproof/microwave-proof container. Heat (double boiler or microwave) until melted.
2. Remove from heat.
3. Stir in almond oil. Mix well.
4. Place bits of crushed dried grapefruit peel inside the molds.
5. Put 2 drops of each essential oil into the molds.
6. Pour the melt mixture into the molds.
7. Set aside for the bath melts to harden fully, in the freezer for 1 hour or a few hours at room temperature.
8. Unmold.
9. Store in a sealed container, away from heat source.

LEMON, GRAPEFRUIT, AND POPPY SEED BATH MELTS

INGREDIENTS:

- 1 oz beeswax
- 1/2 oz shea butter
- 1 oz cocoa butter
- 1/2 oz jojoba oil
- 15 drops grapefruit essential oil
- 15 drops lemon essential oil
- Poppy seeds

DIRECTIONS:

1. Place cocoa butter, beeswax, and shea butter in a heatproof/microwave-proof container. Heat (double boiler or microwave) until melted.
2. Remove from heat.
3. Stir in jojoba oil. Mix well.
4. Stir in the essential oils.
5. Place a few poppy seeds inside the molds.
6. Pour the mixture into the molds.
7. Set aside for the bath melts to harden fully, in the freezer for 1 hour or a few hours at room temperature.
8. Unmold.
9. Store in a sealed container, away from heat source.

CALENDULA BATH MELTS

INGREDIENTS:

- 3.55 oz mango butter
- A few drops bergamot essential oil
- 1/4 tsp annatto seed oil infusion
- 2 tbsp dried calendula petals, finely ground into powder

DIRECTIONS:

1. Place mango butter and calendula powder in a heatproof/microwave-proof container. Heat (double boiler or microwave) until melted.
2. Remove from heat.
3. Stir in the essential oils.
4. Mix in annatto seed oil infusion to give the melt a yellowish tint.
5. Pour the melt mixture into the molds.
6. Set aside for the bath melts to harden fully, in the freezer for 1 hour or a few hours at room temperature.
7. Unmold.
8. Store in a sealed container, away from heat source.

HAPPY SCENT BATH MELTS

INGREDIENTS:

- 150g cocoa butter
- 75ml sweet almond oil
- 15 drops bergamot essential oil
- 15 drops lemon essential oil
- 15 drops grapefruit essential oil

DIRECTIONS:

1. Place cocoa butter in a heatproof/microwave-proof container. Heat (double boiler or microwave) until melted.
2. Remove from heat.
3. Stir in sweet almond oil.
4. Cool the mixture but it should still be liquid.
5. Stir in the essential oils.
6. Pour the melt mixture into the molds.
7. Set aside for the bath melts to harden fully, in the freezer for 1 hour or a few hours at room temperature.
8. Unmold.
9. Store in a sealed container, away from heat source.

CHAPTER 5:

BATH SCRUB AND SALTS RECIPES

COFFEE BATH SCRUB

INGREDIENTS:

- 1/4 cup ground coffee
- 1/4 cup raw sugar
- 2 tbsp coconut oil
- 1 tbsp olive oil
- 1 tbsp sea salt

DIRECTIONS:

1. Mix all the ingredients in a pestle and mortar.
2. Grind all the ingredients together to make a paste.
3. Transfer into a sealable container, like a glass jar with a screw-top lid.

RELAXING LAVENDER-ROSEMARY BATH SALT SCRUB

INGREDIENTS:

- 1/4 cup olive oil
- 1/2 cup kosher salt
- 1 tbsp rosemary leaves, chopped
- 1 tbsp lavender extract, culinary-grade

DIRECTIONS:

1. Mix all the ingredients in a mortar and pestle.
2. Grind all the ingredients together to make a paste.
3. Transfer into a sealable container, like a glass jar with a screw-top lid.

BROWN SUGAR-COCONUT SUGAR SCRUB

INGREDIENTS:

- 2 cups brown sugar
- 1 cup solid but soft coconut oil

DIRECTIONS:

1. Combine all the ingredients until it resembles a coarse dough.
2. Place in a sealed container.

CANDY CANE SUGAR SCRUB

INGREDIENTS:

- 1 cup fine white sugar
- 6 large candy canes
- 15-20 drops peppermint essential oil
- 3/4 cup soft coconut oil

DIRECTIONS:

1. Put the candy cane in a food processor. Pulse to crush into coarse, large pieces.
2. Add the sugar, essential oil, and coconut oil.
3. Pulse until a wet sand/crumbly dough mixture is made.
4. Place in a sealed container.

LAVENDER SUGAR BATH SCRUB

INGREDIENTS:

- 1/2 cup softened coconut oil
- 10-15 drops lavender essential oil
- 2 cups brown sugar
- 2 tsp lavender buds

DIRECTIONS:

1. Mix coconut oil, sugar, and essential oil in a mortar and pestle.
2. Grind all the ingredients together to make a paste.
3. Stir in the lavender buds.
4. Transfer into a sealable container, like a glass jar with a screw-top lid.

LAVENDER-LEMON LAYER BATH SUGAR SCRUB

INGREDIENTS:

- 3 tbsp melted organic coconut oil
- 1 cup granulated sugar
- 10 drops lemon essential oils
- 10 drops lavender essential oils
- 2 drops liquid purple food coloring
- 2 drops liquid yellow food coloring

DIRECTIONS:

1. Cool the coconut oil before adding sugar.
2. Mix well into a dry paste but do not dissolve the sugar.
3. Divide the mixture between 2 bowls.
4. Add lemon essential oil and yellow food coloring to one bowl. Mix well.
5. Add the lavender essential oil and purple food coloring into the other bowl. Mix well.
6. Layer the mixtures in a glass container. Close the lid tightly.

GINGERBREAD SUGAR BATH SCRUB

INGREDIENTS:

- 1 cup coarse sugar
- 3/4 cup solid soft coconut oil
- 2 tbsp molasses
- 1 tsp cinnamon
- 2 tsp ground ginger
- 1/4 tsp ground cloves

DIRECTIONS:

1. Combine all the ingredients until it resembles a coarse dough or wet sand.
2. Place in a sealed container.

HONEY-LEMON BATH SUGAR SCRUB

INGREDIENTS:

- 1 cup sugar
- Juice from 1 lemon
- 1/2 cup olive oil
- 1 tbsp honey

DIRECTIONS:

1. Mix all ingredients in a mortar and pestle.
2. Grind all the ingredients together to make a paste.
3. Transfer into a sealable container, like a glass jar with a screw-top lid.

ALMOND VANILLA SUGAR BATH SCRUB

INGREDIENTS:

- 1/4 cup white sugar
- 1/2 cup brown sugar
- 1/4 cup almond oil
- 3 tbsp vanilla extract

DIRECTIONS:

1. Mix all ingredients in a mortar and pestle.
2. Grind all the ingredients together to make a paste.
3. Transfer into a sealable container, like a glass jar with a screw-top lid.

GINGER COFFEE AND GREEN TEA BATH SCRUB

INGREDIENTS:

- 2 tbsp loose green tea
- 1/2 cup coconut oil
- 1/2 cup un-brewed fresh coffee grounds
- 1/2 cup brown sugar
- 2 tsp ground ginger

DIRECTIONS:

1. Place coconut oil and green tea in a saucepan. Set over low heat until oil melts and starts to simmer. Allow to simmer for 30 minutes.
2. Strain out the tea leaves. Leave to cool.
3. Add sugar, coffee grounds, and ground ginger into the cooled oil mixture.
4. Grind all the ingredients together to make a paste.
5. Transfer into a sealable container, like a glass jar with a screw-top lid.

BUBBLE BATH SALTS

INGREDIENTS:

- 1/2 cup Epsom salt
- 1/2 cup pink Himalayan salt
- 1/2 tbsp liquid Bubble bath
- Soap sprinkles

DIRECTIONS:

1. Combine all the ingredients.
2. Place in a sealed container.

WILD ROSE BATH SALT

INGREDIENTS:

- 2 cups medium grain dead sea salt
- 2 cups medium-sized pink Sea salt

- 7 ml wild rose fragrance oil
- Jasmine flowers
- Pink rose petals

DIRECTIONS:

1. Combine all the ingredients. When adding the essential oils, use a dropper.
2. Mix until the essential oil is evenly distributed.
3. Place in a sealed container.

ORANGE-LAVENDER BATH SALTS

INGREDIENTS:

- 1/2 cup baking soda
- 1/2 cup sea salt
- 2 cups Epsom salt
- 8 drops lavender essential oils
- 8 drops orange essential oils
- 15 drops blue food coloring

DIRECTIONS:

1. Mix the salts and baking soda.
2. Add the essential oils, dropping in different locations around the mixture for a more even mixing.
3. Mix everything well.
4. Add the soap colorant, by dropping in different places for a more even blending of the color.
5. Mix well.
6. Place in a sealed container.

VANILLA-EUCALYPTUS BATH SALTS

INGREDIENTS:

- 1/2 cup baking soda
- 1 cup Epsom salt
- 8 drops vanilla in jojoba oil
- 3 drops eucalyptus essential oil
- 5 drops green food coloring

DIRECTIONS:

1. Mix the salt and baking soda.
2. Add the essential oils, dropping in different locations around the mixture for a more even mixing.
3. Mix everything well.
4. Add the colorant, by dropping in different places for a more even blending of the color.
5. Mix well.
6. Place in a sealed container.

ROSE MILK LUXURIOUS BATH SALT

INGREDIENTS:

- 1/2 cup Epsom salt
- 1 1/2 cups powdered milk, full fat or nonfat
- 1/4 cup dried rose petals
- 5-7 drops rose essential oil
- 2-3 drops red food coloring

DIRECTIONS:

1. Mix the salt and milk.
2. Add the red coloring.
3. Mix well to get a uniform color.
4. Mix in rose petals and essential oil.
5. Mix everything well.
6. Place in a sealed container.

RAINBOW BATH SALT

INGREDIENTS:

- 1 cup sea salt
- 1 cup Epsom salt
- 1/4 cup baking soda
- 1 drop mint essential oil
- 1 drop lavender essential oil
- 1 drop orange essential oil
- 1 drop grapefruit essential oil
- 1 drop green food coloring
- 1 drop purple food coloring
- 1 drop red food coloring
- 1 drop yellow food coloring

DIRECTIONS:

1. Mix the salts and baking soda. Break any lumps.
2. Divide the mixture between 4 bowls.
3. Add the coloring into each bowl.
4. Mix each well.
5. Add the essential oils into each bowl: mint for the green mixture, lavender for the purple, orange for the yellow mixture, and grapefruit for the red mixture.
6. Mix well.
7. Layer the different colored mixtures in a glass container to create a rainbow effect.

ANTI-AGEING ARGAN AND ROSEHIP SEED OIL BATH SALT

INGREDIENTS:

- 1/2 cup baking soda
- 1 cup Epsom salt
- 5-10 drops rosehip seed oil
- 1 tbsp argan oil

DIRECTIONS:

1. Mix the salt and baking soda. Break any lumps.
2. Add rosehip seed oil.
3. Mix well.
4. Stir in argan oil.
5. Mix well.
6. Scoop into a sealable glass container.

CINNAMON ROSE BATH SALT

INGREDIENTS:

- 1 cup coarse sea salt
- 1 tbsp cinnamon powder
- 1/4 cup rose petals

DIRECTIONS:

1. Combine all the ingredients.
2. Place in a sealed container.

AROMATHERAPY BACK PAIN SOOTHING BATH SALT

INGREDIENTS:

- 1 cup baking soda
- 2 cups Epsom salts
- 10 drops peppermint essential oil
- 5 drops cinnamon essential oil
- 5 drops rosemary essential oil
- 5 drops eucalyptus essential oil
- 5 drops lavender essential oil
- 1 tbsp fresh rosemary sprigs
- 2 tbsp dried lavender flowers

DIRECTIONS:

1. Mix the salt and baking soda. Break any lumps.
2. Add the essential oils.
3. Mix well.
4. Stir in dried herbs.
5. Mix well.
6. Scoop into a sealable glass container.

TROPICAL MOJITO MINT BATH SALTS

INGREDIENTS:

- 2 cups sea salt
- Zest and juice of 1 lime
- Fresh mint leaves, diced finely
- 3-5 drops peppermint essential oil

DIRECTIONS:

1. Mix the salt, lime juice, zest, and mint leaves.
2. Add the essential oil.
3. Mix well.
4. Scoop into a sealable glass container.

CHAPTER 6:

BATH TEA RECIPES

COOLING ROSE-SOOTHING CHAMOMILE HERBAL BATH TEA

INGREDIENTS:

- 1 cup dried rose blossom buds or petals
- 2 cups dried chamomile flowers,
- 2 cups dried comfrey leaves, broken
- 1 cup dried lavender flowers
- 12 large sealable tea bags

DIRECTIONS:

1. Mix all the herbs in a large cup. Stir while crushing the herbs to release the oils and aroma.
2. Scoop about 1/2 cup of the herb mix into each tea bag.
3. Seal the tea bags.
4. Store in a sealed container.
5. Drop tea bag in a bathtub then fill with hot water.
6. Steep for a few minutes.

LAVENDER & CHAMOMILE GOAT MILK BATH TEA

INGREDIENTS:

- 3 tbsp powdered goat milk
- 2 tbsp colloidal oatmeal
- 2 tbsp grade 1 lavender buds
- 5 tbsp extra fine Epsom salt
- 20 drops chamomile essential oil
- 40 drops lavender 40/42 essential oil
- Droppers
- 5 large sealable tea bags

DIRECTIONS:

1. Mix Epsom salt, chamomile, and lavender essential oil thoroughly in a bowl.
2. Stir in the milk. Break up all clumps as you mix.
3. Add the lavender buds and colloidal oatmeal.
4. Mix well.
5. Scoop into tea bags.
6. Store in a sealed container.

SILKY OAT BATH TEA

INGREDIENTS:

- 1/4 cup dried lavender buds
- 1 cup oat flour
- 2-3 tbsp shaved cacao butter

DIRECTIONS:

1. Mix all ingredients well in a bowl.
2. Scoop into teabags and seal.
3. Store in sealed container.

PINK LEMONADE TUB TEA

INGREDIENTS:

- 1 1/2 cups Epsom salt
- 1/2 cup Himalayan sea salt
- 1/2 cup ground oatmeal
- 1/2 cup organic dried hibiscus petals
- 6 tbsp organic dried lemon peel
- 20 drops lemon essential oil
- 10 drops grapefruit essential oil
- 5 drops bergamot essential oil
- 1 tsp beet powder

DIRECTIONS:

1. Mix salts, petals, oatmeal, and peel.
2. Add the color. Mix well.
3. Mix in the essential oils.
4. Scoop into tea bags and seal.
5. Store in sealed container.

SWEET SCENT LUXURY BATH TEA

INGREDIENTS:

- 2 tbsp dried rose petals
- 1/2 cup ground almonds
- 3 tbsp dried lavender flower

DIRECTIONS:

1. Mix everything.
2. Scoop into tea bags.

RELAXING BATH TEA

INGREDIENTS:

- 2 tbsp dried chamomile flowers
- 2 tbsp linden flowers
- 1/2 cup ground almonds

DIRECTIONS:

1. Mix everything.
2. Scoop into tea bags.

REJUVENATING BATH TEA

INGREDIENTS:

- 1 tbsp dried lemon verbena leaves
- 2 tbsp dried rosemary
- 1/2 cup cornmeal

DIRECTIONS:

1. Mix everything.
2. Scoop into tea bags.

REFRESHINGLY DEODORIZING BATH TEA

INGREDIENTS:

- 1 tbsp dried lovage root
- 4 tbsp dried peppermint leaves
- 1/2 cup cornmeal

DIRECTIONS:

1. Mix everything.
2. Scoop into tea bags.

CALMING HERBAL BLEND BATH TEA

INGREDIENTS:

- 1 lb Epsom salt
- 1/2 cup chamomile flowers
- 3/4 cup dried lavender buds
- 1/4 cup oatstraw
- 1/4 cup dried peppermint leaves
- 1/4 cup dried rosemary

DIRECTIONS:

1. Mix everything.
2. Scoop into tea bags.

SKIN-SOOTHING BATH TEA

INGREDIENTS:

- 1/8 cup lavender buds
- 1/8 cup calendula buds
- 1/8 cup chamomile buds
- 2 cups sea salt
- 1/2 cup powdered milk
- 1 cup baking soda
- 15-20 drops chamomile essential oils

DIRECTIONS:

1. Mix everything.
2. Scoop into tea bags.

PINK LEMONADE TUB TEA

INGREDIENTS:

- 1/2 cup Himalayan sea salt
- 1 1/2 cups Epsom salt
- 1/2 cup ground oatmeal
- 6 tbsp dried organic lemon peel
- 1/2 cup dried organic hibiscus petals
- 20 drops lemon essential oil
- 5 drops bergamot essential oil
- 10 drops grapefruit essential oil
- 1 tsp beet powder

DIRECTIONS:

1. Mix everything.
2. Scoop into tea bags.

SOOTHING BATH TEA

INGREDIENTS:

- 1 quart water
- 15g dried lavender buds
- 15g dried lemon balm leaves
- 15g dried rose petals

DIRECTIONS:

1. Boil water.
2. Put all the dried herbs in a large mixing bowl.
3. Pour the boiling water over the herbs.
4. Cover the bowl.
5. Steep the herbs for 20 minutes or longer for stronger tea.
6. Strain the tea.
7. Add the tea into a tub full of warm bath water.

CHAPTER 7:

BATH BITS FOR KIDS

CALMING BATH BOMB

INGREDIENTS:

- 1/2 cup baking soda
- 1/4 cup citric acid
- 1/4 cup corn starch
- 20 drops lavender essential oil
- 1 tsp olive oil

DIRECTIONS:

1. Put baking soda, cornstarch, and citric acid in the mixing bowl. Mix well.
2. Add essential oil and olive oil into the mix. Combine well to mix the ingredients evenly.
3. Lightly spray the mixture once then mix well. Check the consistency. Add another spray gradually as needed to achieve the right wet sand consistency.
4. Pack the mixture into the chosen mold. Allow to dry at least overnight. Once completely dry, carefully remove from the mold.

DETOX BATH BOMB

INGREDIENTS:

- 1 cup baking soda
- 1/2 cup citric acid
- 1/2 cup Epsom salts
- 1/2 cup corn starch
- 5-6 drops chamomile essential oils
- 2 tbsp melted coconut oil
- 1-2 tbsp water

DIRECTIONS:

1. Mix all the dry ingredients in a bowl.
2. Mix in coconut oil slowly. Break down any lumps.
3. Add essential oil to the bowl.
4. Add water in small amounts. Mix well after each addition.
5. Check the consistency. Adjust to get the right wet sand form.
6. Pack the mixtures into the mold.
7. Unmold.
8. Allow to dry overnight.
9. Store in a sealed container.

FIZZING HALLOWEEN BATH BOMBS

INGREDIENTS:

- 1/2 cup cornstarch
- 1 cup baking soda
- 1/2 cup Epsom salts
- 1/2 cup citric acid
- 2 tsp coconut oil
- 12 drops lavender essential oil
- Green mica powder
- Water in a spray bottle
- Googly eyes

DIRECTIONS:

1. Mix all the dry ingredients, including the colorant in a bowl thoroughly.
2. Mix in essential oil.
3. Spray the mixture with water. Mix well after each spray.
4. Check the consistency. Adjust to get the right wet sand form.
5. Put the googly eyes into the mold before placing the bath bomb mixture.
6. Pack the mold tightly.
7. Press the two halves of the mold tightly together. Set aside to dry.
8. Allow to dry overnight.
9. Unmold.
10. Store in a sealed container.

RAINBOW SPRINKLES AND COTTON CANDY BATH BOMB

INGREDIENTS:

- 1 cup baking soda
- 1/2 cup cornstarch
- 1/2 cup Epsom salt
- 1/2 cup citric acid
- 2 tsp cotton candy fragrance oil
- 3 tsp water, plus more as needed
- 2-5 drops pink food coloring
- Rainbow nonpareils/ sprinkles

DIRECTIONS:

1. Mix all the dry ingredients well.
2. In a separate bowl, mix all the liquid ingredients.
3. Slowly pour the liquid mixture into the dry mixture while continuously stirring.
4. Mix well and check consistency.
5. Add a drop of water to get the right consistency.
6. Put rainbow sprinkles into the mold.
7. Pack the molds tightly with the mixture.
8. Press the two halves of the mold tightly together.
9. Set aside to dry for 24 hours.
10. Unmold.

SLEEPY APPLE BATH BOMBS

INGREDIENTS:

- 1 cup baking soda
- 3/4 cup cornstarch
- 1/2 cup Epsom salt
- 1/2 cup citric acid
- 1 tbsp fractionated coconut oil
- 10 drops green food coloring
- 10 drops apple fragrance oil
- Water in a spray bottle

DIRECTIONS:

1. Mix all the dry ingredients in a bowl.
2. In a separate bowl, mix all the liquid ingredients.
3. Slowly pour the liquid mixture into the dry mixture while continuously stirring.
4. Mix well.
5. Check consistency.
6. Add small sprays of water as needed to get the right consistency.
7. Pack the molds tightly with the mixture.
8. Press the two halves of the mold tightly together.
9. Unmold.
10. Set aside to dry overnight.

MAGIC GROW ANIMAL BATH BOMBS

INGREDIENTS:

- 1 cup baking soda
- 1/2 cup citric acid
- 1/2 cup corn starch
- 1/2 cup Epsom Salt
- 2 drops yellow food coloring
- 2 tsp roman chamomile essential oil
- 3 tsp water
- 1 magic grow animal pills
- Water in a spray bottle

DIRECTIONS:

1. Mix all the dry ingredients well.
2. In a separate bowl, mix all the liquid ingredients.
3. Slowly pour the liquid mixture into the dry mixture while continuously stirring.
4. Mix well. Check consistency.
5. Add small sprays of water as needed to get the right consistency.
6. Pack one of the molds halfway with the bath bomb mixture. Press 1 magic grow animal pills into the mold. Cover the rest of the mold with the mixture.
7. Fill the other half of the mold.
8. Press the two halves of the mold tightly together. Set aside to dry for 24 hours.
9. Unmold.

MICKEY ORANGE SCENTED BATH BOMBS

INGREDIENTS:

- 1 cup baking soda
- 1/2 cup sea salt
- 1/2 cup cornstarch
- 1/2 cup citric acid
- 1 tbsp vegetable oil
- 3/4 tsp essential oils
- Water in a spray bottle

DIRECTIONS:

1. Mix all the dry ingredients well.
2. In a separate bowl, mix all the liquid ingredients.
3. Slowly pour the liquid mixture into the dry mixture while continuously stirring.
4. Mix well.
5. Check consistency.
6. Pack the mouse molds tightly with the mixture.
7. Set aside to dry for 24 hours.
8. Unmold.

BUBBLE GUM BATH BOMBS

INGREDIENTS:

- 2 cups baking soda
- 1/4 cup cornstarch
- 1 cup citric acid
- 2 tbsp Epsom salts
- 1 tsp polysorbate 80
- 1/3 cup melted coconut oil
- 1 tsp bubble gum scented oil
- 1 tsp biodegradable cosmetic glitter
- 1 tbsp pink mica powder
- 1 tbsp edible pink sugar pearls

DIRECTIONS:

1. Mix all the dry ingredients, except glitter, sugar pearls, and mica powder.
2. In a separate bowl, mix all the liquid ingredients.
3. Slowly pour the liquid mixture into the dry mixture while continuously stirring.
4. Break down any lumps.
5. Mix well.
6. Stir in cosmetic glitter and mica powder.
7. Mix well.
8. Put sugar pearls into the mold.
9. Fill the molds loosely but overfilled with the mixture.
10. Press the two halves of the mold tightly together.
11. Unmold.
12. Set aside to dry for 24 hours.

SPIDER HERO BATH BOMB

INGREDIENTS:

- 1/4 cup dead sea salts
- 2 cups baking soda
- 1/4 cup cornstarch
- 1 cup citric acid
- 1 tbsp polysorbate 80
- 1/3 cup melted coconut oil, plus more for decorating
- 2 drops red food coloring
- 1 tsp candy apple scented oil
- Black mica powder
- Red and black biodegradable cosmetic glitter
- Rubbing alcohol in a spray bottle
- Spider web silicone mold

DIRECTIONS:

1. Mix all the dry ingredients, except glitter, well.
2. In a separate bowl, mix all the liquid ingredients.
3. Slowly pour the liquid mixture into the dry mixture while continuously stirring.
4. Mix well.
5. Add the red food color.
6. Mix well.
7. Pack the mixtures into the mold.
8. Set aside to dry for 24-48 hours.
9. Unmold.
10. Melt the additional coconut oil. Brush the oil lightly all over the bath bomb.
11. Paint the surface with red and black glitter.
12. Let it dry.
13. Store in a sealed container.

CHAPTER 8:

BATH BITS FOR HIM

MINT PINE BATH BOMBS

INGREDIENTS:

- 3 tbsp Epsom salt
- 1 cup baking soda
- 1/2 cup corn starch
- 1/2 cup citric acid
- 1 tbsp coconut oil
- 5-8 drops pine essential oil
- 5-8 drops mint essential oil
- Green food coloring
- Witch hazel in a spray bottle

DIRECTIONS:

1. Mix all the dry ingredients in a bowl.
2. Mix in coconut oil slowly. Break down any lumps.
3. Add essential oils to the bowl.
4. Mix well
5. Add the coloring. Mix well.
6. Spray 5 times with witch hazel.
7. Mix well and check consistency.
8. Add small sprays as needed to get the right consistency.
9. Fill the molds loosely but overfilled with the mixture.
10. Press the two halves of the mold tightly together.
11. Allow to dry overnight.

12. Unmold.
13. Store in a sealed container.

ROUGH-AND-RUGGED BATH BOMBS

INGREDIENTS:

- 1/2 cup baking soda
- 1/2 cup citric acid
- 1/2 cup Epsom salts
- 5 drops cedarwood essential oil
- 5 drops mint essential oil
- 2 drops rosemary essential oil
- 5 drops lemon essential oil
- 5 drops sandalwood essential oil
- Water in a spray bottle

DIRECTIONS:

1. Mix all the dry ingredients well.
2. Stir in all the essential oils.
3. Mix well to evenly distribute the oil throughout the mixture.
4. Spray once with water. Mix well and check consistency. Add small sprays as needed to get the right consistency.
5. Pack the molds tightly with the mixture.
6. Press the two halves of the mold tightly together. Set aside to dry.
7. Unmold.

COFFEE BATH BOMBS

INGREDIENTS:

- 1 cup baking soda
- 1/2 cup citric acid
- 1/2 cup corn starch
- 1/4 cup Epsom salt
- 2-3 tbsp freshly ground coffee
- 1 tbsp almond oil
- Water in a spray bottle
- 3 coffee beans for each bath bomb to decorate

DIRECTIONS:

1. Mix all the dry ingredients, including the ground coffee. Break down any lumps.
2. Stir in the almond oil.
3. Mix well to evenly distribute the oil throughout the mixture.
4. Spray once with water. Mix well and check consistency. Add small sprays as needed to get the right consistency.
5. Place 3 coffee beans on one of the molds.
6. Fill both molds with the mixture.
7. Press the two halves of the mold tightly together. Set aside to dry.
8. Unmold.

VALOR BATH BOMBS

INGREDIENTS:

- 1/2 cup citric acid
- 1 cup baking soda
- 1/2 cup Epsom salt
- 1/2 cup arrowroot flour,
- 2 1/2 tbsp sweet almond oil
- 20-25 drops of sandalwood essential oil
- Water in a spray bottle
- Brown food coloring

DIRECTIONS:

1. Mix all the dry ingredients, including pigment powder well.
2. In a separate bowl, mix all the liquid ingredients.
3. Slowly pour the liquid mixture into the dry mixture while continuously stirring.
4. Mix well.
5. Check consistency.
6. Adjust with a small spray of water if the mixture is too dry to hold its shape.
7. Fill the molds loosely but overfilled with the mixture.
8. Press the two halves of the mold tightly together.
9. Carefully remove half of the mold.
10. Set aside to dry for 6-8 hours.
11. Remove the other half of the mold.
12. Allow to sit and dry for another hour.
13. Store in a sealed container.

SEAWEED, GREEN TEA, AND EPSOM SALT BATH BOMB

INGREDIENTS:

- 1/4 cup Epsom salt
- 1 cup baking soda
- 1/2 cup cornstarch
- 1/2 cup citric acid
- 1 tbsp dried green tea
- 2 tbsp seaweed powder
- 2 tbsp castor oil
- 6 drops lemongrass essential oil
- 6 drops lemon essential oil
- 6 drops ginger essential oil
- Water in a spray bottle

DIRECTIONS:

1. Mix all the dry ingredients in a bowl.
2. Mix in castor oil slowly. Break down any lumps.
3. Add essential oils to the bowl, one drop at a time. Mix well after each addition.
4. Check the consistency.
5. Adjust to get the right wet sand form by adding a small amount of more castor oil or preferred essential oil.
6. Fill the molds loosely but overfilled with the mixture.
7. Unmold.
8. Allow to dry overnight.
9. Store in a sealed container.

ARAME BATH BOMB

INGREDIENTS:

- 1/2 cup baking soda
- 1/4 cup cornstarch
- 1/4 cup citric acid
- 1/4 cup combination of fine and coarse sea salt
- 1 tbsp arame seaweed
- 1 tbsp almond oil
- 15 drops juniper berry essential oil
- Blue food coloring

DIRECTIONS:

1. Mix all the dry ingredients, except seaweed, well.
2. Add essential oils to the bowl, one drop at a time. Mix well after each addition.
3. Set aside a few tablespoons of the mixture in another bowl.
4. Add blue colorant to the mixture in this new bowl. Add drop by drop, mixing well after each addition.
5. Crush the seaweed and add to the blue mixture. Mix well.
6. Fill one half of the bath bomb mold with the blue mixture.
7. Fill the other half with the white mixture.
8. Fill the molds loosely but overfilled with the mixture.
9. Press the two halves of the mold tightly together. Set aside to dry.
10. Unmold.
11. Store in a sealed container.

BIG BLUE BATH BOMB

INGREDIENTS:

- 2 cups baking soda
- 1-2 tbsp cornstarch
- 1 cup citric acid
- 3/4 cup dried seaweed
- 1/4 cup olive oil
- 0.30 oz island fragrance oil
- 10-15 drops miracle glow oil

DIRECTIONS:

1. Mix all the dry ingredients well.
2. Stir in the essential oil drop by drop. Mix well after each addition.
3. Mix well to evenly distribute the oil throughout the mixture.
4. Slowly pour the olive oil into the mixture, mixing constantly. Stop once a wet sand consistency is achieved.
5. Stir in the seaweed.
6. Fill the molds loosely but overfilled with the mixture.
7. Press the two halves of the mold tightly together.
8. Set aside to dry for 24 hours.
9. Unmold.

MINT CHOCOLATE BATH BOMB

INGREDIENTS:

- 1 cup baking soda
- 2/3 cup citric acid
- 2/3 cup sea salt
- 1/3 cup SLSa (Sodium Lauryl Sulfoacetate)
- 1/3 colloidal oatmeal
- 2/3 cup melted cocoa butter
- 1o drops peppermint essential oil
- 5 drops lemon essential oil

DIRECTIONS:

1. Mix all the dry ingredients well.
2. Stir in the essential oil drop by drop. Mix well after each addition.
3. Mix well to evenly distribute the oil throughout the mixture.
4. Slowly pour the melted cocoa butter into the mixture, mixing constantly. Stop once a wet sand consistency is achieved.
5. Fill the molds loosely but overfilled with the mixture.
6. Press the two halves of the mold tightly together.
7. Set aside to dry for 24 hours.
8. Unmold.

MAHOGANY BATH BOMBS

INGREDIENTS:

- 1/2 cup cornstarch
- 1/8 cup activated charcoal
- 3 tbsp MSM powder
- 1/4 cup Epsom salt
- 1 cup baking soda
- 3/4 citric acid
- 1 tbsp walnut oil
- 1 tbsp mahogany oil
- 1 tbsp cocoa butter
- 1 tbsp shea butter

DIRECTIONS:

1. Mix all the dry ingredients thoroughly.
2. Melt the butters.
3. Stir in the oils into the melted butters.
4. Slowly pour butter-oil mixture into the dry mixture. Combine thoroughly.
5. Check the consistency.
6. Pack the mixture into the mold tightly. Allow to dry for 24 hours before removing.
7. Place bombs in a sealed container and allow to dry fully.

MOISTURIZING BATH BOMBS

INGREDIENTS:

- 1/2 cup cornstarch
- 1/4 cup Epsom salt
- 1 cup baking soda
- 3/4 citric acid
- 1 tbsp jojoba oil
- 1 tbsp avocado oil
- 1 tbsp cocoa butter
- 1 tbsp shea butter
- 1 tbsp mango butter

DIRECTIONS:

1. Mix all the dry ingredients thoroughly.
2. Melt the butters.
3. Stir in the oils into the melted butters.
4. Slowly pour butter-oil mixture into the dry mixture, mixing continuously. Stop when consistency resembles wet sand.
5. Pack the mixture into the mold tightly. Allow to dry for 24 hours before removing.
6. Place bombs in a sealed container and allow to dry fully.

CONCLUSION

I'd like to thank you and congratulate you for transiting my lines from start to finish.

I hope this book was able to help you to gain a better understanding about bath bombs, melts, salts, and scrubs. Making your own is easy. You have these recipes with the simplest 2-3 ingredients to more luxurious ones with added skin-friendly ingredients to level up your bath.

The next step is to start trying out these recipes. Make your bath more fun and enjoyable. You can give these as great gifts. You may even use these recipes to start your own business, who knows?

I wish you the best of luck!

Made in United States
North Haven, CT
09 February 2023

32287234R10070